T0152474

FINDING HOPE in HARDSHIP

"People are desperate for hope filled with love that strengthens, peace that remains in the storm, and joy that does not fade in difficult circumstances. In this uplifting book, Shonn exposes the hopeful truths of the Philippian letter and brings alive the pathway to hope. If you need encouragement look no further than *Finding Hope in Hardship*."

Dr. Anthony Jordan
Executive Director/Treasurer,
Baptist General Convention of Oklahoma
Oklahoma City, Oklahoma

"Prisons fail to top the list of places where one looks for hope, yet the words of the Apostle Paul, written from jail, remind us that hope is forward-looking and future-acting. In *Finding Hope in Hardship*, Shonn challenges us to be hope dispensers, especially amid conflict and chaos. May his words inspire and encourage you to walk in love and move in hope!"

Dr. Keith Newman
President, Southern Nazarene University
Bethany, Oklahoma

"The book of Philippians is a letter filled with hope during extreme trials. Shonn captures the hope-filled spirit of the letter in this book and presents it in a careful and compelling fashion. Perhaps, *Finding Hope in Hardship* is needed more today than any other time in our history."

Cesar Arocha
Senior Pastor, Dallas Bay Church
Hixson, Tennessee

"We are living in unprecedented times. Economic instability, the cries of injustice, the effects of a global pandemic, rising unemployment rates, and the diminishing numbers of the American Evangelical Church consistently fill the news. Many are experiencing hardship in their homes today. Shonn gives us an answer in *Finding Hope in Hardship*. I encourage you to read, digest, and live out the principles in this great book."

Chip Minton
International Evangelist
2-Time U.S. Olympian and WCW Wrestler, Retired
Pensacola, Florida

"Paul, in the book of Philippians, gives a clear message of encouragement to believers, centered on Christ, to empower them through the Holy Spirit to rest in Him and live for Him. Shonn takes the reader through the study of this book to discover, practically, how to dig deeper in his faith to develop a healthy, humble, hearty, and hopeful mind in order to align one's thinking with God's perspective."

Jim Shorter
Senior Pastor, ChristPoint Church
Florence, South Carolina

"I once heard Shonn say, 'Don't look at problems as problems! Look at them as challenges to overcome!' The truth is, what some see as obstacles that hinder, others see as hurdles of opportunity. Shonn, in *Finding Hope in Hardship*, seeks to emulate the truth Paul exemplifies in encouraging Christians to identify with Jesus Christ regardless of their circumstances. There is hope in the midst of the dark days of life! Shonn encourages the reader to search, identify, and live out the true joy that comes with a life sold out to Jesus. Shonn is an encourager! As you read this commentary, you will be encouraged to seek God at all cost!"

David Williams
Senior Pastor, Temple Baptist Church
Moss Point, Mississippi

FINDING
HOPE in
HARDSHIP

Lessons for Life from the
Book of Philippians

SHONN KEELS

NASHVILLE

NEW YORK • LONDON • MELBOURNE • VANCOUVER

FINDING HOPE in HARDSHIP
Lessons for Life from the Book of Philippians

© 2022 SHONN KEELS

Published in New York, New York, by Morgan James Publishing. Morgan James is a trademark of Morgan James, LLC. www.MorganJamesPublishing.com

Proudly distributed by Ingram Publisher Services.

A **FREE** ebook edition is available for you or a friend with the purchase of this print book.

CLEARLY SIGN YOUR NAME ABOVE

Instructions to claim your free ebook edition:
1. Visit MorganJamesBOGO.com
2. Sign your name CLEARLY in the space above
3. Complete the form and submit a photo of this entire page
4. You or your friend can download the ebook to your preferred device

ISBN 978-1-63195-673-7 paperback
ISBN 978-1-63195-674-4 ebook
Library of Congress Control Number: 2021911494

Cover Design by:
Rachel Lopez
www.r2cdesign.com

Morgan James is a proud partner of Habitat for Humanity Peninsula and Greater Williamsburg. Partners in building since 2006.

Get involved today! Visit MorganJamesPublishing.com/giving-back

TABLE OF CONTENTS

ACKNOWLEDGMENTS

Thank you, Bonnie, for standing by my side since May 22, 1993. You are God's biggest blessing in my life. I am forever grateful you said "yes." You model well the lessons included in this book. You are no stranger to pain; yet, because of your great love for Jesus, you have no problem *Finding Hope in Hardship*.

Ryleigh Watson, thank you for serving as my editor. You have a sharp eye, a keen sense for excellence, and a big heart.

David Hancock, you and the team at Morgan James Publishing are a true blessing. Thank you for believing in me as an author and for being the best publisher and the best publishing company, I know.

FOREWORD

With the heart of a pastor, mind of a scholar and discipline of an athlete, Shonn Keels provides this most timely and practical resource based on his uniquely personal insights gleaned from the apostle Paul's letter to the church at Philippi. As the effects of the global pandemic continue unabated, Shonn skillfully guides the reader through the lessons taught us by the apostle who faced his own daunting challenges at Philippi yet miraculously experienced God's peace and joy through them all. Our understanding and application of these lessons and the principles that emanate from them will most certainly help us as we navigate our own current set of trials. Your faith will be encouraged, mind challenged, and heart strengthened as you read and apply these most pertinent lessons from this uniquely helpful book.

One of life in the ministry's great honors lies with relationships built during this journey of service. One of those highlights for me was the time spent serving with Shonn Keels and his precious family. Shonn, because of his military and athletic background, possesses a rare ability to effectively relate to a wide array of people of which I observed him do with great regularity. Additionally, Shonn does all this with both a humble spirit and a bold witness for our Lord. Through the years God has allowed our paths to cross from time to time and each time I have come away enriched and refreshed. As you read this book, I believe your experience will be the same.

Jim Austin
Dr. Jim Austin
Executive Director/Treasurer,
South Carolina Baptist Convention, Retired
Columbia, South Carolina

PREFACE

I finished my Doctor of Ministry degree at the beginning of the 2020 global pandemic. After completing the degree, I sensed the Lord stirring in my heart to use the time I normally spend studying to continue writing books that would honor Him and build people. Because of this stirring from the Lord, I was compelled to write this book on the letter of Philippians, during these unsettling times, as an encouragement to those of us in search of *Finding Hope in Hardship*.

The ongoing unexpected threat of COVID-19 is significantly changing the world around us. Hospitals are overcrowded. Death and despair are ubiquitous. Unemployment is at an all time high. People are losing their jobs, businesses are closing down, and churches are shutting their doors. Simultaneously, the cries of injustice are growing in the streets, and the threat of civil violence is commonplace. In the midst of the chaos, "new normal" is the new mantra; yet it is not normal at all. We are living in unprecedented times and for many of us, **hardship is our reality!**

Together, we will learn in Paul's letter to the Philippian church, joy in the midst of personal pain is possible. Paul writes from a prison in Rome where he is incarcerated for preaching the gospel of Jesus. His desire is to help people, not hurt people. Paul wants nothing more than to introduce people to the unchanging and incomparable love of God found in Christ Jesus; yet he is imprisoned for his benevolent desire to serve humanity. While in prison, Paul does not wallow in self-pity; nor does he whine about his current situation. Instead, Paul finds joy in the midst of his prison sentence. As we examine his life and dissect this letter, we discover *Finding Hope in Hardship* is possible for those of us who have the right perspective.

Sitting in a prison, most people look up and see cell bars, not Paul; he chooses to see the stars. Why the difference? Paul has an amazing perspective on life. His perspective makes all the difference. Because of Paul's eternal perspective, he discovers joy in the midst of pain, purpose in the midst of persecution, opportunity in the midst of opposition, and hope in his hardship. You, too, can have this joy!

As we study this ancient letter together, may God give us an eternal perspective, and as we press forward in uncertainty may *Finding Hope in Hardship* become our "new normal."

INTRODUCTION

Life without pain is impossible. Everyday people like you and me experience hurt and heartache. Disappointment and despair are strangers to no one. Doing everything right, if that were even possible, does not promise us a life devoid of trials and tribulations. The fact is, in life, everyone will face some kind of hardship. Be encouraged; Jordan Easley writes, "Impossible circumstances are where God's glory shines the brightest."[1] This is what the book of Philippians is all about. The apostle Paul demonstrates and encourages us that *Finding Hope in Hardship* is possible.

The apostle Paul, along with some friends on his second missionary journey, start a church in the ancient city of Philippi. Together, Paul and his friends build a generous and faithful church in about three months. Paul's time in Philippi marks the beginning of his ministry in Macedonia.

---

1   Jordan Easley. "Facebook Post", Dec. 5. Pastor First Baptist Church, Cleveland, Tennessee, 2020.

His ministry throughout Macedonia is a result of a vision he receives in the city of Troas. Troas is located across the northeastern corner of the Aegean Sea from Neapolis, a neighboring port city of Philippi (Acts 16:8-40). Led by the Holy Spirit, Paul and his companions bear much fruit in Philippi.

During their brief stay in Philippi, Paul and his companions build a core of people hungry for the gospel and the work of the ministry. Among the early members were Lydia, a sharp businesswoman who gladly opens her home to Paul and his co-laborers (Acts 16:13-5), and a Philippian jailer, who surrenders his life to Christ under Paul's influence after an earthquake miraculously breaks open the prison doors (Acts 16:22-34). The jailer, Lydia, and the people who join them quickly grow to love and support Paul. After receiving news about Paul being held in a prison in Rome for spreading the gospel of Jesus, this young church takes up an offering to help assist him in his ministry. A member of the church named Epaphroditus takes Paul this gift and a report on the state of the church. Paul receives the gift and the report with gladness in spite of his own personal hardship and later sends Epaphroditus back to Philippi with a letter, the book of Philippians.

Paul likely writes this letter as the latest of his four prison epistles in AD 61 or 62. Earlier he writes Ephesians, Colossians, and Philemon and sends them by Tychicus to their recipients because their destinations were in close proximity to one another. As previously mentioned, Epaphroditus delivers the Philippian letter to Paul (Phil. 2:25; 4:18). It is important to note, while in Rome, Epaphroditus gets sick, which delays his return home and the delivery of the letter (Phil. 2:26-27). However, these men are undeterred by the challenges surrounding them. They press forward in spite of these hardships. Their highest aim is to make Christ known. Paul writes, "The important thing is that in every way, whether from false motives or true, Christ is preached. And because of this I rejoice" (Phil. 1:18).

Paul's mantra can be summed up in one verse, "To live is Christ and to die is gain" (Phil. 1:21). **His perspective is unquestionable; it is all about Jesus.** Paul's conviction concerning the future of the Philippians is clear, "… he who began a good work in you will carry it on to completion until the day of Christ Jesus" (Phil. 1:6). Paul is confident that God will continue the work He started in his friends. He knows God will not forsake His children. He also encourages his friends that in Christ, they will have the strength needed to face any circumstance (Phil. 4:13), and their needs will always be met for the glory of God (Phil. 4:19).

In this brief letter, Paul shares a heartfelt message with his friends. The message is overflowing with great joy in spite of Paul's difficult circumstances. It is clear, Paul desires for the Philippian church to experience this same joy. In

Paul's message, we discover lessons of how *Finding Hope in Hardship* is possible. While his life is a shining example of how to turn troubles into triumphs, discouragement into encouragement, and stumbling blocks into steppingstones, Paul gives them the greatest testimony of an overcomer by pointing them to Jesus (Phil. 2:5-11). Jesus is the greatest example of perseverance in spite of pain. He is the ultimate example of obedience in the face of opposition. Paul points out how Jesus' most painful tragedy is His greatest triumph. The Lord's example impacts Paul's witness and his words. Paul's life and his message are meant to encourage the Philippians to gain a new perspective. They should also move us to change our thinking from a temporal perspective to an eternal one. Applying the lessons we learn in this book will help us live with a greater level of joy and serve with a greater level of confidence.

I pray God will allow each of us to find the same joy Paul and his friends experience. I also pray this joy will lead us to avoid unnecessary disputes within our churches and keep us devoid of division within the family of faith. May God grant us a humble spirit and a heavenly perspective. And may our chief aim be to know Christ and make Him known.

Chapter One

A HEALTHY MIND

Philippians 1:1-11

Paul and Timothy, servants of Christ Jesus,

To all God's holy people in Christ Jesus at Philippi, together with the overseers and deacons:

2Grace and peace to you from God our Father and the Lord Jesus Christ.

3I thank my God every time I remember you. 4In all my prayers for all of you, I always pray with joy 5because of your partnership in the gospel from the first day until now, 6being confident of this, that he who began a good work in you will carry it on to completion until the day of Christ Jesus.

7It is right for me to feel this way about all of you, since I have you in my heart and, whether I am in chains or defending and confirming the gospel, all of you share in God's grace with me. 8God can testify how I long for all of you with the affection of Christ Jesus.

9And this is my prayer: that your love may abound more and more in knowledge and depth of insight, 10so that you may be able to discern what is best and may be pure and blameless for the day of Christ, 11filled with the fruit of righteousness that comes through Jesus Christ—to the glory and praise of God.

Lesson One: *Finding Hope in Hardship* comes from joyfully praying for others.

In the beginning of this brief letter, Paul begins with a joyful prayer for others. This may seem odd to many considering Paul is serving a sentence in a Roman jail for preaching the gospel of Jesus and his impending death is on the horizon. Nevertheless, Paul does joyfully respond in his unfortunate circumstance. His healthy perspective enables him to live with a laser focus on what matters most in life—others. Thinking of others, especially in times of personal difficulty, can ease your pain. Psychological research reveals that altruistic behavior promotes healing for the hurting. Psychologist Karl Menninger writes, "Love cures people—both the ones who give it and the ones who receive it."[2] Focusing on others lessens the pain. **The one who possesses a healthy mind glorifies God and is good to others**.

Read again the following verses. Take special notice of Paul's attitude and the content of his prayer. Also remember, Paul is writing from a prison.

> *3I thank my God every time I remember you. 4In all my prayers for all of you, I always pray with joy 5because of your partnership in the gospel from the first day until now, 6being confident of this, that he who began a good work in you will carry it on to completion until the day of Christ Jesus.*
>
> *7It is right for me to feel this way about all of you, since I have you in my heart and, whether I am in chains or defending and confirming the gospel, all of you share in God's grace with me. 8God can testify how I long for all of you with the affection of Christ Jesus.*

In spite of his circumstances, Paul joyfully turns to praying for others rather than complaining about his own

---

2   Karl A. Menninger. "Inspiring Quotes", (https://www. inspiringquotes.us/author/5136-karl-a-menninger).

hardship. Paul makes a choice to see the good in what could come out of his circumstances rather than concentrating on the bad that surrounded him. Praying for others helps him joyfully make this choice. The people in Philippi matter deeply to Paul. His love for the Philippians leads him to prayer which fills him with hope even in his hardship.

Today, praying for others seems to be a lost art for those who claim to love Jesus especially when they are experiencing a hardship. Believers, when faced with difficulty, are more likely to complain or ask "why" instead of praying for others. Even when life is good, some Christians spend more time checking the status of each of their social media platforms than they do praying for others. According to Paul's example, this cannot be the norm for those desiring to find hope in hardship. Charles Spurgeon agrees, "Neglect of private prayer is the locust which devours the strength of the church."[3] Believers need to make prayer a priority. This includes you and me. We can no longer neglect praying for others. Nehemiah writes, "The joy of the Lord is my strength" (Neh. 8:10). This joy will come to us even in the darkest hour if we are faithful to make praying for others of paramount importance on our list of things to do each day. **Praying for others must become our first response and not our last resort.**

---

3   Charles Haddon Spurgeon. "Spurgeon at His Best: Over 2200 Striking Quotations from the World's Most Exhaustive and Widely read Sermon Series." Baker Publishing Group, 1988.

Paul is thankful for his friends in Philippi. He is especially thankful for their partnership in the gospel ministry (v5). The word partnership comes from a Greek word which means fellowship. However, the word partnership has a much deeper meaning than how we in the church tend to think of fellowship today. Often, fellowship is used in the context of sharing a meal or getting together to play a game. While there is nothing inherently wrong with either of these activities, one can share a meal or play a game without experiencing the type of fellowship Paul writes about in this verse. The fellowship Paul is writing about means "a shared life." Paul is literally saying to the believers in Philippi, he thanks God because they are fellow recipients of God's amazing grace. As fellow recipients of grace, they share in the responsibility of spreading this gospel of grace to others. They are partners! This is also true of us. In Christ, we are partners. Indeed, we are family and family shares in privilege and responsibility. All believers share in this partnership as recipients of grace and representatives of the gospel. **Let us be sure to express our thankfulness for our spiritual family and the partnership we have in Christ regularly as we pray for others.**

The next part of this chapter reveals some important ingredients that are included in Paul's prayer for his friends. The content of his prayer is a key in understanding the importance of how we should pray for others. Carefully reread verses nine through eleven.

> *9And this is my prayer: that your love may abound more and more in knowledge and depth of insight, 10so that you may be able to discern what is best and may be pure and blameless for the day of Christ, 11filled with the fruit of righteousness that comes through Jesus Christ—to the glory and praise of God.*

Notice, Paul is very specific in his prayer for the Philippian church. He lists three things in which he petitions God for on behalf of his friends. He prays they will be filled with love, grow in character, and devote themselves to service. Let us learn from Paul's prayer.

The first thing Paul prays is that their "… love may abound more and more …" (v9). Love is the most defining characteristic of a Christ follower. The apostle John declares, "… God is love" (1 Jn. 4:8). Because God is love, we too, are called to live a life of love. John also writes, love compelled God to provide the way of salvation for mankind, "For God so loved the world that he gave his one and only Son, that whoever believes in him shall not perish but have eternal life" (Jn. 3:16). The apostle Paul adds, God demonstrated this love even while we were still in our sin (Rom. 5:8). This sacrificial love is to be the most defining characteristic of Christians. Paul prays this for his friends in Philippi. He asks God to increase their love for each other. Paul knows their love for each other will serve as a testimony to others that they are indeed God's children. John concurs, "We know that we have passed from death to life, because we love each other" (1 Jn. 3:14). Christian love is what binds us together. When we demonstrate this kind of love, we paint a picture for the world of what God looks like. As the old song goes, they will know we are Christians because we love one another. When we truly love each other as God loves us, we are faithful in our witness.

The second thing included in Paul's prayer indicates, a true demonstration of this love will increase the ability of his friends to discern between what is good and what is best. Paul prays, "… so that you may be able to discern what is best and may be pure and blameless for the day of Christ …" (v10). This level of discernment will help build the type of Christian character God desires for His children. According to Paul's prayer, when we love like God loves, we will make the type of choices reflective of who we are in Him. When we love like God loves, we will pass over what is simply good and choose what is best. Paul's prayer indicates the growing Christian can discern between good and bad. His prayer also indicates, we really need God's help in discerning between what is good for us and what is best for us. Bad is easy to recognize; most believers have no problems recognizing the bad things in life. However, the difference between good and best is more challenging to discern. This is why Paul prays for his friends to possess the ability to discern between what is good from what is pure and blameless. The difference between good and best is much more difficult to discern. We need God's help. When we love like God loves, choosing what is best is possible.

Finally, Paul's prays for his friends to be devoted in service to the Lord. He prays, the Philippians will be "… filled with the fruit of righteousness that comes through Jesus Christ—to the glory and praise of God …" (v11). Take special notice, the type of service Paul prays for is only possible when one is truly walking with the Lord Jesus daily. He clearly writes, the "fruit" comes through Jesus Christ. The apostle John agrees, "Remain in me, as I also remain in you. No branch can bear fruit by itself; it must remain in the vine. Neither can you bear fruit unless you remain in me" (Jn. 15:4). Producing fruit is impossible apart from possessing faithfulness. Paul literally prays for his friends to walk closely with Jesus daily and for this close walk with the Lord to produce a life of service to others. In his letter to the church in Ephesus Paul writes, all believers are made for a life of service. "For we are God's workmanship, created in Christ Jesus to do good works, which God prepared in advance for us to do" (Eph. 2:10). We are made to serve God by giving away our lives in service to one another. This life of service is a natural overflow from an intimate and growing walk with Jesus.

Consider the following example: in Acts chapter three, Peter and John heading to pray, heal a lame man. The crowds ask by what authority is the man healed. Peter and John use this as an opportunity to share the gospel of the Lord Jesus with the onlookers. This benevolent act of service lands Peter and John before the authorities who are angry and astonished at the words and the witness of these two men. Luke writes, "When they saw the courage of Peter and John and realized that they were unschooled and ordinary men, they were astonished, and they took note that these men had been with Jesus" (Acts 4:13). Notice what gave these men the courage and the capability to speak and serve with such power, "... these men had been with Jesus" (Acts 4:13). Jesus made the difference in their lives and He will do the same for you and me. If we are faithful to walk with Jesus each day, He will fill us with the power to produce such fruit. Our faithfulness honors God and attracts people.

A non-believer may argue about many things when it comes to belief in God. He may argue about the historical accuracy of the Scriptures or claim the Bible is not truly God's Word. However, the unbeliever cannot argue about a believer's faithful testimony. A testimony filled with a deep love for others, strong character, and the willingness to serve others even in times of personal difficulty, this is something an unbeliever simply cannot deny. Jesus agrees, "… let your light shine before others, that they may see your good deeds and glorify your Father in heaven" (Mt. 5:16). A solid Christian testimony is what God often uses to lead the unbeliever to salvation and what Paul prays for in this passage. May God strengthen us all to possess such love, character, and service for His glory! Then we are on our way to *Finding Hope in Hardship*.

Lesson Two: *Finding Hope in Hardship* comes from living life with a higher perspective.

Philippians 1:12-26

12Now I want you to know, brothers and sisters, that what has happened to me has actually served to advance the gospel. 13As a result, it has become clear throughout the whole palace guard and to everyone else that I am in chains for Christ. 14And because of my chains, most of the brothers and sisters have become confident in the Lord and dare all the more to proclaim the gospel without fear.

15It is true that some preach Christ out of envy and rivalry, but others out of goodwill. 16The latter do so out of love, knowing that I am put here for the defense of the gospel. 17The former preach Christ out of selfish ambition, not sincerely, supposing that they can stir up trouble for me while I am in chains.

18But what does it matter? The important thing is that in every way, whether from false motives or true, Christ is preached. And because of this I rejoice.

Yes, and I will continue to rejoice, 19for I know that through your prayers and God's provision of the Spirit of Jesus Christ what has happened to me will turn out for my deliverance. 20I eagerly expect and hope that I will in no way be ashamed, but will have sufficient courage so that now as always Christ will be exalted in my body, whether by life or by death. 21For to me, to live is Christ and to die is gain. 22If I am to go on living in the body, this will mean fruitful labor for me. Yet what shall I choose? I do not know! 23I am torn between the two: I desire to depart and be with Christ, which is better by far; 24but it is more necessary for you that I remain in the body. 25Convinced of this, I know that I will remain, and I will continue with all of you for your progress and joy in the faith, 26so that through my being with you again your boasting in Christ Jesus will abound on account of me.

One of Paul's greatest wishes is to take the gospel to Rome (Acts 19:21). Paul understands Rome is the greatest city in the ancient world. If he can infect Rome with the gospel, it would soon spread to the whole world. He is so excited to take the gospel to Rome he writes, "That is why

I am so eager to preach the gospel to you who are in Rome" (Rom. 1:15). He sets out on his journey to visit Rome as a preacher and instead enters the great city as a prisoner. Paul sets out on a conquest; yet he is convicted as a criminal. He longs for a spiritual triumph; yet he receives an unexpected tragedy. Paul expects to overcome any opposition to the gospel and preach freely among the Romans; yet there are a few obstacles which make his movement about the city impossible. Nevertheless, Paul looks to a higher purpose in his painful position. This heavenly perspective leads him to *Finding Hope in Hardship*.

Look again at what Paul writes, "Now I want you to know, brothers and sisters, that what has happened to me has actually served to advance the gospel" (v12). Paul sees his situation as a blessing. His eternal perspective enables him to find hope in an incredible hardship. Rather than revering Paul as a wonderful preacher of the gospel, he is received as a wretched prisoner. However, Paul makes a choice to look above his situation and capitalize on his surroundings. Paul uses three things he is surrounded by to find hope in his hardship. He uses his shackles, his scoffers, and his situation for the sake of the gospel. These three things are meant to stifle his ministry; yet they propel his ministry forward. Similar to what happened in Joseph's life (Gen. 50:20), what others meant to destroy Paul's ministry God uses for good to accomplish His plan.

Now look again at verses twelve through fourteen:

12Now I want you to know, brothers and sisters, that what has happened to me has actually served to advance the gospel. 13As a result, it has become clear throughout the whole palace guard and to everyone else that I am in chains for Christ. 14And because of my chains, most of the brothers and sisters have become confident in the Lord and dare all the more to proclaim the gospel without fear.

First, Paul uses his shackles to turn his hardship into hope. The shackles are meant to halt the spread of the gospel; instead they help the spread of the gospel. How? Paul's perspective makes the difference. Because Paul chooses to see a higher purpose in his stay in prison, fellow Christians are now boldly proclaiming the gospel. Paul's perspective helps turn a presumed stumbling block into a steppingstone. The prison is now a platform. What is meant to decelerate Paul's mission is accelerating his ministry. While in shackles, Paul is fervently preaching the gospel throughout the whole palace guard (v13). Fellow believers who were once silent in their witness are now boldly sharing the gospel everywhere (v14). There is a silver lining in hardship if we look in the right place. God is always at work in the lives of those who love Him (Rom. 8:28).

What shackles are holding you back? These shackles may be the very thing God uses to set you up for a higher purpose. Overcoming obstacles is not always easy; however, overcoming them is always possible. Jesus agrees, "With man this is impossible, but with God all things are possible" (Mt. 19:26). **Perspective is often what makes the difference between the impossible and the possible.** Paul looks at his shackles with an eternal perspective. Let me encourage you with God's help to do the same. *Finding Hope in Hardship* is often a matter of the mind. This is why Paul exhorts us to maintain the right perspective (Col. 3:1-2).

Look at verses fifteen through eighteen again.

> *15It is true that some preach Christ out of envy and rivalry, but others out of goodwill. 16The latter do so out of love, knowing that I am put here for the defense of the gospel. 17The former preach Christ out of selfish ambition, not sincerely, supposing that they can stir up trouble for me while I am in chains. 18But what does it matter? The important thing is that in every way, whether from false motives or true, Christ is preached. And because of this I rejoice.*

Secondly, Paul uses his scoffers to turn his hardship into hope. Notice in the above verses, some are now preaching Christ for the right reasons. Paul's example stirs them to boldly share the good news of Jesus with others. However, among them are a group of scoffers. These scoffers are preaching Christ for all the wrong reasons with the goal of stirring up trouble for Paul (v17). Paul's critics are operating in direct opposition to his mission of making Christ known in Rome and throughout the world. Yet, Paul takes the high road and chooses to believe that even his opposition is an opportunity for the gospel to spread for the glory of God (v18). **Perspective is paramount for *Finding Hope in Hardship*.** Paul shows us this with his life and shares this with us in his letter.

Let the actions of Paul concerning his scoffers soak in a minute. Seriously, criticism is a tough pill for any of us to swallow especially when living in the middle of unfavorable circumstances. To add insult to injury, many of Paul's critics are claiming to be among the family of God—the very people Paul dearly loves. This had to hurt him deeply. Malcolm Tolbert writes, "To be misunderstood by his brothers was a source of greater pain than the hatred of the gospel's enemies."[4] Opposition from outside the camp stings; but pain from the opposition inside the camp is severe. However, Paul's single-minded devotion to the Lord Jesus and making Him known enables him to find hope in his hardship (Acts 20:24). Perhaps when the scoffers come our way, we would do better to ask "How" rather than "Why." "God how can I serve you in this storm?"; rather than, "Why is this happening to me?" Please help us O' Lord!

---

4   Malcolm Tolbert. *Layman's Bible Book Commentary: Philippians*, volume 22, Nashville, Tennessee: Broadman Press, 1980: 19.

Before we continue, please read again the following verses:

> *19for I know that through your prayers and God's provision of the Spirit of Jesus Christ what has happened to me will turn out for my deliverance. 20I eagerly expect and hope that I will in no way be ashamed, but will have sufficient courage so that now as always Christ will be exalted in my body, whether by life or by death. 21For to me, to live is Christ and to die is gain. 22If I am to go on living in the body, this will mean fruitful labor for me. Yet what shall I choose? I do not know! 23I am torn between the two: I desire to depart and be with Christ, which is better by far; 24but it is more necessary for you that I remain in the body. 25Convinced of this, I know that I will remain, and I will continue with all of you for your progress and joy in the faith, 26so that through my being with you again your boasting in Christ Jesus will abound on account of me.*

Finally, Paul uses his situation to demonstrate hope in hardship is possible. Understanding his death could be imminent and that he may never see his friends face-to-face again, Paul writes, his greatest ambition is to be with Christ whether in his life or in his death. Paul does not fear death; he actually prefers it. However, he knows the choice between life and death is not his to make. This choice is the responsibility of God. Because of this, Paul assures his friends, he is all right in his current situation as long as he can continue to make a difference with his life and witness. Paul is single-minded in his love for Jesus and his service to others for the sake of the gospel. He points out how the growing faith of his friends add to his joy. Remember, we too can experience this joy when we realize our current situation may be for someone's salvation. As Paul wraps up this thought, he teaches the importance of partnership. Friends, we are all in this together!

Lesson Three: *Finding Hope in Hardship* is possible for those who allow their biblically driven beliefs to drive their everyday behavior.

Philippians 1:27-30

27Whatever happens, conduct yourselves in a manner worthy of the gospel of Christ. Then, whether I come and see you or only hear about you in my absence, I will know that you stand firm in the one Spirit, striving together as one for the faith of the gospel 28without being frightened in any way by those who oppose you. This is a sign to them that they will be destroyed, but that you will be saved—and that by God. 29For it has been granted to you on behalf of Christ not only to believe in him, but also to suffer for him, 30since you are going through the same struggle you saw I had, and now hear that I still have.

In the final verses of chapter one, Paul encourages his friends in Philippi to do three things as they move forward in life and ministry: he encourages them to live with a deep conviction, serve in purpose-driven community, and to walk in the confidence which comes from knowing Christ personally. Paul makes clear in this chapter; the Christian life is not a playground. He warns them that the Christian life is a battleground filled with opposition (Phil. 1:28). This warning is common in Paul's letters to the churches (Eph. 6:12). He regularly warns his readers to be prepared for the spiritual battle. Paul assures the Philippians, along with this warning, they do not have to be frightened (v28). Let me also assure you with God's Word, as you face your own battles, "Be strong and very courageous. Do not be afraid; do not be discouraged, for the LORD your God will be with you wherever you go" (Josh. 1:9). Just as Paul assures his friends, so God's Word assures us. The promise given to Joshua is also good for us!

First, in verse twenty-seven, Paul encourages his Philippian friends to live a life of conviction, and he reminds them this conviction will flow out of a life devoted to the gospel. It is a fact: one's belief affects one's behavior. If we are to heed Paul's encouragement, we must spend time studying the Scriptures. Our conviction will grow as we spend time studying God's Word and sharing the gospel of Christ (Heb 5:14). King David adds, memorizing the Scriptures will also help us live lives worthy of Christ Jesus (Ps. 119:11). It is impossible to live with conviction apart from the study of God's Word. Years ago, I heard a preacher say, **"A dusty Bible leads to a dirty life."** This is TRUTH! We need to dust our Bibles off to clean up our lives.

A missionary excitedly makes his trek deeper into the jungle with only a backpack filled with a few necessities and one copy of God's Word in the native language of the tribe he is visiting. This is the first copy of the Bible to be translated for this tribe. At this time, very few missionaries have made visits this far into the jungle. This is new territory for the advancement of the gospel. After a few weeks of fruitful ministry, the missionary leaves the copy of the Bible with one of the young converts. The young man promises to take good care of the Bible. After several months, the missionary returns to find the young man with only a few thin portions of the Bible in his possession. The missionary is disappointed and inquires why the Bible is torn into smaller portions. The young man explains that he was not careless with the Bible; instead, he divided it into sections so others would have some of God's Word to read. After new Christians would read a section, they would pass it along to others. The young man explains, he could not be selfish with the Bible. He believes it is so good; he just had to share it with others. May God give us such a love for His Word. This affection for the Scriptures will serve as a fountain for deep conviction.

Secondly, in verse twenty-seven, Paul continues that his friends should stand firm together as they move forward living for Jesus and sharing the gospel. They are to be one in the Spirit and one in purpose. **A cooperative partnership is necessary for the church and its members to thrive**. Moving forward together will make an eternal difference. We should take notice of this encouragement. This is how we are going to change our world—**TOGETHER!** This is also how we will find hope in our hardships— **TOGETHER!**

Finally, in these closing verses of chapter one, Paul encourages his friends to walk with confidence as they are sure to face opposition. This is reminiscent of Jesus' encouragement to His disciples, "In this world you will have trouble. But take heart! I have overcome the world" (Jn. 16:33). Troubles will come; but we do not fight them alone (Heb. 13:5). We also do not fight for victory; we fight from victory (1 Cor. 15:55-57). The Lord Jesus has conquered sin, death, Hell, and the grave. **Because He lives, we have victory in Him!** Knowing this to be true, we can face each day with the confidence that Paul prays for his friends in Philippi to possess. Let me encourage you to pause for a few moments and meditate on Romans chapter eight verses thirty-one through thirty-nine (Rom.

8:31-39). Now, walk with confidence knowing that Jesus has your six all the time.

Response to Chapter One: (What will you do to develop a healthy mind?)

1. Read Romans 12:1-2. What will you do daily to develop an eternal perspective?

   _____

   _____

   _____

   _____

2. Read 2 Corinthians 10:5. What will you do with any negative thoughts that arise in your mind?

   _____

   _____

   _____

   _____

3. Read Colossians 3:1-2. How will this change what you allow to enter your mind?

   _____

   _____

   _____

   _____

4. Read Jeremiah 33:3. How will this impact your prayer life?

   _____

   _____

   _____

   _____

5. Read Joshua 1:8. How will this impact your personal time of studying the Scriptures?

_____

_____

_____

_____

Chapter Two

A HUMBLE MIND

Philippians 2:1-11

1 Therefore if you have any encouragement from being united with Christ, if any comfort from his love, if any common sharing in the Spirit, if any tenderness and compassion, 2then make my joy complete by being like-minded, having the same love, being one in spirit and of one mind. 3Do nothing out of selfish ambition or vain conceit. Rather, in humility value others above yourselves, 4not looking to your own interests but each of you to the interests of the others.

5In your relationships with one another, have the same mindset as Christ Jesus:

6Who, being in very nature God,
did not consider equality with God something to be used to his own advantage;

7rather, he made himself nothing
by taking the very nature of a servant,
being made in human likeness.

8And being found in appearance as a man,
he humbled himself
by becoming obedient to death—
even death on a cross!

9Therefore God exalted him to the highest place
and gave him the name that is above every name,

10that at the name of Jesus every knee should bow,

in heaven and on earth and under the earth,

11and every tongue acknowledge that Jesus Christ is Lord,

to the glory of God the Father.

As we begin chapter two, let me encourage you to spend time with the Lord in prayer. This is a tough; but extremely rewarding chapter, especially this first section. In this section, Paul addresses the news he receives about some internal and external strife (Phil. 3:1-3; 4:1-3). False teachers are infiltrating the ranks and there is bickering among the membership. This cannot happen if the church is to fulfill her redemptive potential. Therefore, Paul calls his friends to live with a humble mind. He exhorts his friends to be selfless, servants, sacrificial, and saintly. **Demonstrating a humble mind leads to helping others and honoring God!**

Lesson One: *Finding Hope in Hardship* comes from humble mind and a selfless attitude.

In this section, Paul exhorts his friends to be selfless, "Do nothing out of selfish ambition or vain conceit. Rather, in humility value others above yourselves, not looking to your own interests but each of you to the interests of the others" (2:3-4). Surely this was in response to the public disagreement between Euodia and Syntyche (4:1-3). Disagreements? Do church people ever disagree? Hah! You and I both know the family of God is not devoid of arguments, disagreements, and in some cases, fighting. The old saying appears to be true, "To live above with saints we love, now this will be glory; but to dwell below with the saints we know, now this is another story!" **Relationships can be a challenge and the relationships in the church can be even more challenging**. However, as Paul reminds the Philippians, we are to be selfless in our relationships especially in the church. Literally, we are to think of others and their needs before we consider our own (v4). Humility is to be the hallmark of every Christian. One man says,

"Humility is not thinking less of yourself; it is not thinking of yourself at all." Wow! That's difficult to swallow; yet it is necessary if we are to walk in humility. Like I mentioned earlier, this section is a tough one.

Lesson Two: *Finding Hope in Hardship* comes from living a life of service to others.

Paul continues as he exhorts his friends to be servants, "In your relationships with one another, have the same mindset as Christ Jesus: Who, being in very nature God, did not consider equality with God something to be used to his own advantage; rather, he made himself nothing by taking the very nature of a servant, being made in human likeness (2:5-7). This is both rich and righteous. Read these verses again. "In your relationships with one another, have the same mindset as Christ Jesus: Who, being in very nature God, did not consider equality with God something to be used to his own advantage; rather, he made himself nothing by taking the very nature of a servant, being made in human likeness" (2:5-7). Paul exhorts his friends to be a servant like Jesus and uses the illustration of His incarnation to communicate what it really means to serve others. Ponder and pray on this truth for a minute! Seriously, the Son of God who is God leaves heaven and comes to earth forfeiting His divine rights literally becoming a human to live among mankind in a fallen world for the sole purpose of serving His creation (Mt. 20:28). This is mind boggling! This is the very definition of a servant! Jesus gives up everything to become like you and me as the ultimate act of service. **This, Paul says, is to be our main ambition—to be like Christ the servant!**

Mr. Willie is a great older man. One day he walks into my office, tells me he wants to serve in the church, but due to his age, he can only offer prayer and trash pick-up as long as we can provide him with a trash can that has wheels on the bottom. First, I tell Mr. Willie his offering of prayer and trash pick-up is a great offering and assure him his ministry is vital to the success of our mission to reach and grow people across the street and around the world in the name of the Lord Jesus Christ. Mr. Willie smiles and then prays the most heartfelt prayer over our church and me. He then meets with our facilities manager, gets a proper trash can, and begins going room-to-room collecting our trash from the weekend. He did this every Tuesday for a long time. I always look forward to him stopping by and praying over me. Most never knew Mr. Willie did these acts of service. This is a modern-day picture of humble service.

Lesson Three: *Finding Hope in Hardship* **comes from living a life of sacrifice.**

The Lord Jesus says, "It is more blessed to give than to receive" (Acts 20:35). While this may sound like an oxymoron, it is one of the greatest paradoxes in the

Christian faith. Giving equals receiving and sacrifice equals reward. On a side note, we can never outgive the inexhaustible kindness of God. This is the message Paul communicates to his friends in the next verse, "And being found in appearance as a man, he humbled himself by becoming obedient to death—even death on a cross" (2:8)! Jesus gives His all. Paul points out how Jesus sacrifices His own will for the will of the Father. He demonstrates obedience to pay the ultimate price for the sin of the world (Mk. 14:36). This level of obedience takes great sacrifice. Paul tells his friends this is what real service looks like. **It can be easy to give out of our plenty; yet God calls us to give even when it hurts.** If our service to others does not result in sacrifice, it is less likely that it will accomplish much. We must live a life of sacrifice. It is in our sacrifice that we look the most like Jesus! It is in our sacrifice that *Finding Hope in Hardship* is made possible.

A recently discharged Marine, a man who is no stranger to sacrifice, learns of a young adult lady about his age who needs a live liver transplant. Without hesitation and not knowing her, the Marine volunteers to give away half of his liver so this lady can live. Because a healthy liver can regenerate, the Marine and the young lady both have a shot at a normal life. They meet, begin to get to know each other, the surgery takes place, and they both live happily ever after. Seriously, they live happily ever after. Let me explain. During this time, the Marine is dealing with making a shift back to civilian life. Having made this adjustment myself, I understand that the transition can be very tough. However, the Marine's time spent with the young lady and his willingness to offer such a great sacrifice gives him hope in his hardship. While spending time together, these two strangers develop a unique bond which eventually leads them to the altar. Today, they not only have regenerated livers, they are married and have a beautiful family. They both find joy in the midst of pain and their lives testify, *Finding Hope in Hardship* **is made possible when we live a life of sacrifice**. The joy filled life comes through sacrifice. Lord, help us to sacrificially give our lives to you in service to others for your glory and the good of your Kingdom.

Lesson Four: *Finding Hope in Hardship* comes from living a saintly life.

To live a saintly life literally means to live a holy life. Paul writes in verses nine through eleven that Jesus' humiliation led to His exultation. This is true of us too! When we humbly live in obedience to God, He promises a future reward. James writes, "Humble yourselves before the Lord, and he will lift you up (Js. 4:10). Paul uses Jesus' example to encourage his friends to live saintly lives. This encouragement includes the hope that comes from saintly living—victoriously reigning with the Lord Jesus in His future Kingdom! Oh, Lord please help us to honor You.

Help us to be selfless, to serve others, to sacrifice, and to live saintly lives.

Philippians 2:12-18

12Therefore, my dear friends, as you have always obeyed—not only in my presence, but now much more in my absence—continue to work out your salvation with fear and trembling, 13for it is God who works in you to will and to act in order to fulfill his good purpose.

14Do everything without grumbling or arguing, 15so that you may become blameless and pure, "children of God without fault in a warped and crooked generation." Then you will shine among them like stars in the sky 16as you hold firmly to the word of life. And then I will be able to boast on the day of Christ that I did not run or labor in vain. 17But even if I am being poured out like a drink offering on the sacrifice and service coming from your faith, I am glad and rejoice with all of you. 18So you too should be glad and rejoice with me.

Lesson One: *Finding Hope in Hardship* comes from pursuing God's purpose.

Developing a humble spirit does not come without its challenges especially when living among difficult people. Yet, Paul challenges his friends to do this even though there is bickering among the ranks and opposition against their community of faith. In this brief section of chapter two, Paul includes three challenges sure to help his friends build humble spirits. He challenges his friends: to pursue God's purpose, to live in God's power, and to walk in God's promises.

Paul begins this section with a challenge for his friends to continue to work out their salvation with fear and trembling (2:12). This is God's purpose for the people who make up the church at Philippi, and this is God's purpose for us. **All believers in every generation are called to work out their own salvation with fear and trembling.** What does this mean—to work out our salvation? Isn't salvation the gift of God (Eph. 2:8-9)? Yes, the Bible is abundantly clear that salvation is the gift of God, and we cannot work for it. So, what does Paul mean, "work out your salvation" (2:12)? First, take note, Paul clearly writes the letter of Philippians to "… God's holy people in Philippi …" (1:1). There is no ambiguity here. Paul writes to those who are already saved through faith in Jesus Christ. Again, what does Paul mean? Notice, Paul did not write "work for your salvation", he writes "work out your salvation" (2:12). Working for something and working out something are two very different things. Consider a puzzle for a moment. If you give me a puzzle for a gift, it is clear that I possess it; yet I did not earn it. The puzzle is a gift. However, just because I receive the puzzle or the gift does not mean it is put together. On the contrary, I have to work to put the puzzle together. The puzzle is a gift; but I must work to get the most out of the gift. Similarly, this is what Paul expresses in verse twelve. Salvation is a gift from God. We cannot earn salvation (Jn. 14:6). However, we are to work diligently to grow in—work out our salvation in order to maximize our redemptive potential. If we simply go through life making no effort to submit to God's purpose for our lives, we will fall short and according to Paul lose rewards when we stand before Jesus (1 Cor. 3:10-15). Paul encourages his friends to make the most of the gift of salvation becoming all God created them to be and so the Bible declares to us. **We are saved to grow and serve with a humble spirit— this is God's purpose for you and me, and this does not happen by accident** (Eph. 2:8-10). We must cooperate with God and work out our salvation.

Lesson Two: *Finding Hope in Hardship* comes to those who live in God's power.

In this section, God also encourages his friends to live in God's power. Paul writes, "for it is God who works in you to will and to act in order to fulfill his good purpose" (2:13). Pursuing God's purpose is only possible when we live in His power. Paul reminds the Philippians of their need to acknowledge and accept God's power for daily living and so the Bible reminds you and me. We cannot faithfully "work out our salvation" apart from the power of God. We need His help.

I remember serving in the mountains of Jamaica in a very poor rural village. On Sunday morning I arrive early at the little Jamaican church with our mission team. We are the only ones sitting in the little block building. After some time, a little old lady arrives, takes her seat, and starts to sing, "I need Jesus in my walking, I need Jesus in my talking, every minute of the day, I need Jesus!" She sings for at least five minutes by herself, over and over again: "I need Jesus in my walking, I need Jesus in my talking, every minute of the day, I need Jesus!" Then, another lady walks in and goes to her seat. Together the two ladies sing, "We need Jesus in our walking, we need Jesus in our talking, every minute of the day, we need Jesus!" After a few minutes, others enter the church and make their way to their seats. The crowd joins the two ladies in singing, "We need Jesus in our walking, we need Jesus in our talking, every minute of the day, we need Jesus!" **Friends, this is what Paul teaches in verse thirteen, we need Jesus!** We cannot fulfill God's good purpose for our lives apart from His help. We need to live in His power! Please remember this cannot happen apart from consistently studying God's word, being devoted to prayer, participating regularly in the gathering together with other believers, and faithfully submitting to the leading of the Holy Spirit throughout each day. Practicing these spiritual disciplines makes living in God's power possible. God's power will make all the difference in your life and mine.

Lesson Three: *Finding Hope in Hardship* comes to those who walk in God's promises.

Finally, in this section, Paul encourages his friends to walk humbly in God's promises. Because belief determines behavior, we need to take God at His word and walk accordingly. Paul shows the Philippians that God promises victories along the way in this life and in the life to come for those who humbly walk according to His promises (2:14-18). In this chapter, Jesus sets the example of demonstrating a humble spirit and receiving victory (2:5-11). In this section, Paul guarantees the same for those who follow Jesus' example (2:14-18). Jesus set the example for us (Heb. 12:1-2). Let us look to His example, take God at His word, and live obediently. Paul writes humble obedience not only brings blessing to our lives, it serves as a testimony to others. When we walk with Jesus, we also shine among the lost and depraved world like the stars in the sky pointing them to Jesus (2:15). The apostle Peter agrees, "Live such good lives among the pagans that, though they accuse you of doing wrong, they may see your good deeds and glorify God on the day he visits us (1Peter 2:12). Help us O' Lord! Help us to walk faithfully in your promises and to make an eternal difference in the lives of others. Help us to possess and exercise a humble spirit. *Finding Hope in Hardship* **is**

possible when we are controlled by a humble mind. This hope is contagious. It will bring blessing to our lives and to those we influence.

Philippians 2:19-30

19I hope in the Lord Jesus to send Timothy to you soon, that I also may be cheered when I receive news about you. 20I have no one else like him, who will show genuine concern for your welfare. 21For everyone looks out for their own interests, not those of Jesus Christ. 22But you know that Timothy has proved himself, because as a son with his father he has served with me in the work of the gospel. 23I hope, therefore, to send him as soon as I see how things go with me. 24And I am confident in the Lord that I myself will come soon.

25But I think it is necessary to send back to you Epaphroditus, my brother, co-worker and fellow soldier, who is also your messenger, whom you sent to take care of my needs. 26For he longs for all of you and is distressed because you heard he was ill. 27Indeed he was ill, and almost died. But God had mercy on him, and not on him only but also on me, to spare me sorrow upon sorrow. 28Therefore I am all the more eager to send him, so that when you see him again you may be glad and I may have less anxiety. 29So then, welcome him in the Lord with great joy,

*and honor people like him, 30because he almost died
for the work of Christ. He risked his life to make up
for the help you yourselves could not give me.*

**Lesson One: *Finding Hope in Hardship* is available
to all believers who are led by a humble mind.**

In the closing section of Philippians chapter two, Paul
uses the example of two ordinary men to show his friends
in Philippi that living with a humble spirit is possible for
every believer, not just the spiritual elite. After pointing
them to Jesus as the perfect example and demonstrating
in his own life what a humble spirit looks like, Paul gives
them the testimonies of Timothy and Epaphroditus. These
two young men are not apostles. The Bible records no
testimony of either of these men performing any miracles.
Timothy and Epaphroditus are considered to be among the
everyday people like you and me. However, Paul uses these
men as illustrations of people who are led by a humble
mind and experience great joy in their lives because of the
same. You too can experience such joy.

Lesson Two: Possessing a humble mind is not
automatic, it is developed intentionally over time and
requires faithfulness.

Timothy learns what it means to walk with Jesus from
an early age watching the witness of his grandmother and
mother (2 Tim. 1:5). He likely becomes a Christian under
the preaching of Paul in his home city of Lystra (Acts 14:6-

7; Phil. 2:22). Paul later refers to Timothy as, "my true son in the faith ..." (1 Tim. 1:2). Again, Paul writes of Timothy, "... my son whom I love, who is faithful in the Lord (1 Cor. 4:17). Many, along with Paul, hold Timothy in high regard for his faithfulness (Acts 16:1-3). Paul writes, "I have no one else like him, who will show genuine concern for your welfare" (Phil. 2:20). **Faithfulness to God's word and God's will is key to developing a humble spirit.** Timothy developed this faithfulness over time. We can also develop such faithfulness. This is an important step in our spiritual journey. Faithfulness is what God requires (1Peter 5:9). If we are going to grow a humble spirit, we must be faithful in our walk and witness even in the face of challenge and chaos. **Faithfulness contributes to our finding joy even in the midst of uncertain times (Phil. 2:19).**

Lesson Three: Possessing a humble mind is not automatic, it is developed intentionally over time and requires availability.

Timothy is not only faithful, he is also available for God's work. Luke writes about how Timothy makes himself available to accompany Paul in his missionary travels (Acts 16:3-5). Timothy's availability for the work of God helps strengthen the church and her evangelistic activity (Acts 16:5). In Philippians Paul reiterates how "... Timothy has proved himself ..." by being available to assist him (2:22). Availability is so important in the Christian life;

Paul writes to Timothy later and encourages him to search for others who are available to help move the mission of God forward (2 Tim. 2:1-7). Availability requires a humble spirit. It requires one to surrender his own will to the very will of God. **Please remember, God is not looking for ability; he is looking for availability**. Like Timothy, if we make ourselves available; God will make us able.

Lesson Four: Possessing a humble mind is not automatic, it is developed intentionally over time. Being controlled by a humble mind may cost us time, energy, resources, and even our health.

Consider Epaphroditus. Paul writes, "But I think it is necessary to send back to you Epaphroditus, my brother, co-worker and fellow soldier, who is also your messenger, whom you sent to take care of my needs. For he longs for all of you and is distressed because you heard he was ill. Indeed he was ill, and almost died" (Phil. 2:25-27a). Notice, Epaphroditus is sick even to the point of death. He sacrificed his health to serve both Paul and the Philippians. He also sacrificed time and energy. Epaphroditus volunteers to take Paul the offering (2:25). This obviously took time and energy. It is likely, Epaphroditus contributes to the very offering he takes to Paul. Either way, it is safe to deduce that Epaphroditus humbles himself greatly to serve Paul and the Philippian church and his humble service causes him great sacrifice and sickness (2:30).

I witnessed this type of humble service, sacrifice, sickness, and joy firsthand. Years ago, my dad accompanied me to Romania on a mission trip. We served small village churches, engaged in some outdoor service projects, did open air evangelism, and led a crusade while in Romania. God honored our ministry, and we witnessed hundreds respond to the gospel. The trip was not without expense to my dad and the other team members. My dad was in his seventies. He had the time to travel; but it cost him more than $1,400 to go on the trip. It also cost him his health. The weather in Romania was very cold and wet. My aged father caught pneumonia and spent some time in the hospital when we returned to the United States. His stay in the hospital also cost him financially. However, because of the humble spirit of my aged father many came to Christ and the faith of the other mission team members was strengthened. Despite the financial sacrifice, the sickness, and his stay in the hospital, my dad received great joy from his time in Romania. Tim Tebow writes, "There's always a reason, however small, to find joy in this day."[5] Yes, no matter the cost, we can find joy each day as we give our lives away in service to others in the name of the Lord Jesus.

---

5   Tim Tebow. "Facebook Post", Dec. 5. Famous Football Player and
      TV personality. 2020.

Lesson Five: Possessing a humble mind makes cooperation more likely and cooperation is necessary for advancing the mission of God.

As earlier mentioned, the church moves forward TOGETHER. We do need each other. As we wrap up this last section of chapter two, Paul points out this truth once again. He writes, "He risked his life to make up for the help you yourselves could not give me (2:30). Paul acknowledges that many in the Philippian church contribute to an offering for him. However, he also points out, not all of them make the trip to Rome to deliver the offering. Paul reminds them, Epaphroditus volunteers and delivers the offering. Paul is refreshed because the church works together. Some give, surely some pray, and Epaphroditus serves as a messenger who delivers a word about the church and an offering. Everybody does their part, and the gospel moves forward. Everybody does their part, and many walk in joy in spite of the hardship that surrounds them. ***Finding Hope in Hardship* is possible when we are controlled by a humble mind in which leads us to move forward in cooperation.**

Response to Chapter Two: (What will you do to develop a humble mind?)

1. Read Matthew 20:20-28. What does this passage teach about humility?

   _____

   _____

   _____

   _____

2. Read Luke 10:25-37. What does this passage teach about service and sacrifice?

   _____

   _____

   _____

   _____

3. Read James 4:10. What does this verse teach about practicing humility?

   _____

   _____

   _____

   _____

4. Read 1 Peter 1:13-16. What do these verses teach about living a surrendered life?

   _____

   _____

   _____

   _____

5. Read Matthew 22:34-40. What does this passage teach concerning how we are to live?

    _____

    _____

    _____

    _____

Chapter Three
A HEARTY MIND

Philippians 3:1-14

1Further, my brothers and sisters, rejoice in the Lord! It is no trouble for me to write the same things to you again, and it is a safeguard for you. 2Watch out for those dogs, those evildoers, those mutilators of the flesh. 3For it is we who are the circumcision, we who serve God by his Spirit, who boast in Christ Jesus, and who put no confidence in the flesh— 4though I myself have reasons for such confidence.

If someone else thinks they have reasons to put confidence in the flesh, I have more: 5circumcised on the eighth day, of the people of Israel, of the tribe of Benjamin, a Hebrew of Hebrews; in regard to the law, a Pharisee; 6as for zeal, persecuting the church; as for righteousness based on the law, faultless.

7But whatever were gains to me I now consider loss for the sake of Christ. 8What is more, I consider everything a loss because of the surpassing worth of knowing Christ Jesus my Lord, for whose sake I have lost all things. I consider them garbage, that I may gain Christ 9and be found in him, not having a righteousness of my own that comes from the law, but that which is through faith in Christ—the righteousness that comes from God on the basis of faith. 10I want to know Christ—yes, to know the power of his resurrection and participation in his sufferings, becoming like him in his death, 11and so, somehow, attaining to the resurrection from the dead.

12Not that I have already obtained all this, or have already arrived at my goal, but I press on to take hold of that for which Christ Jesus took hold of me. 13Brothers and sisters, I do not consider myself yet to have taken hold of it. But one thing I do: Forgetting what is behind and straining toward what is ahead, 14I press on toward the goal to win the prize for which God has called me heavenward in Christ Jesus.

Lesson One: *Finding Hope in Hardship* **comes to those who develop a hearty mind.**

A hearty mind is not automatic; it is developed over time. A hearty mind does not think on outward "things." Heartiness springs from inside a person. In this section, Paul shares one major key concerning the ability to possess such enthusiasm, exuberance, and vigor. And yes, this heartiness springs from having the right perspective concerning "things." Notice, Paul introduces this truth by addressing those among the ranks who put confidence in earthly things (3:1-4). In context, Paul is addressing a false teaching prevalent in his day dealing with circumcision. He writes, "Watch out for those dogs, those evildoers, those mutilators of the flesh" (v2). These men claim circumcision of the flesh is necessary for one to truly be a Christian. Paul clears up any confusion concerning this false teaching, "For it is we who are the circumcision, we who serve God by his Spirit, who boast in Christ Jesus, and who put no confidence in the flesh ..." (v3). Notice Paul teaches salvation is in Christ and it does not come from earthly "things." Salvation cannot be earned. Paul possesses the spiritual pedigree necessary to brag if the false teachers' message is true (vv4-6). However, their message is not true. Paul continues, whatever he has done, is doing, or will do is nothing compared to truly knowing God through faith in Christ (vv7-9). Paul clarifies, peace with God is only possible through a growing intimate relationship with Jesus Christ (vv10-11).

Today, there are also false teachers in the American evangelical church. There are many who teach salvation comes through faith in Jesus Christ and obedience to certain sacraments. Others proclaim that knowing God is possible if you believe in Jesus and do good things. While doing good is not a bad thing, we cannot do enough good to earn salvation. Salvation is only possible through faith in Christ (Eph. 2:8-9). While there is nothing inherently wrong in the keeping of certain sacraments, keeping them will not result in salvation. We simply cannot do anything to earn salvation. Be wise! Weigh everything you hear concerning the Lord with what God has already given us in the Scriptures (Acts 17:11). If God says it, then it is true. But if it is not in God's word, it is pure heresy. **Remember, God's word will never fail**! The Bible contains the answers to our questions. It contains the instructions we need for life and godliness. As the old preacher writes, "Show me a Bible that's falling apart, and I will show you a life that's not." Open your Bible daily and allow God to strengthen you each day.

Lesson Two: Possessing a hearty mind comes from living with a little holy dissatisfaction.

In the next piece of this section, Paul changes gears from salvation to sanctification. He moves from discussing how we come to know Christ personally to how we are to live in a perpetual pursuit of growing in Christ. He uses his own personal example to model for us how we should never become complacent in our spiritual journey, "Not that I have already obtained all this, or have already arrived at my goal, but I press on to take hold of that for which Christ Jesus took hold of me. Brothers and sisters, I do not consider myself yet to have taken hold of it" (vv12-13a). Even though Paul possesses a hearty perspective, one filled with unbelievable joy; he lives with a level of holy dissatisfaction. Paul knows there is more he can do for the Lord, and there is more God wants to do in and through him (vv13b-14). This level of righteous dissatisfaction drives Paul to press forward. May we never become satisfied with where we are in our spiritual journey; but may we always be satisfied with whose we are as a child of God.

Lesson Three: Possessing a hearty mind comes from a proper understanding of things.

The key to this section is found at the end. Paul writes, "But one thing I do: Forgetting what is behind and straining toward what is ahead, I press on toward the goal to win the prize for which God has called me heavenward in Christ Jesus" (vv13b-14). Paul says, his earthly achievements and accolades mean absolutely nothing to him anymore. He continues with what is most important in life, eternal things. It is about priority. Yesterday is gone. Living in light of eternity must be a priority today. As one preacher writes, "We have but one life to live and it will soon be past, only what is done for Christ will last." If we are to maximize our redemptive potential, we must develop a heavenly perspective (Col. 3:1-2) and make living for Jesus a priority today (Lk. 9:23). The consistent pursuit of the eternal instead of the temporal will help you develop a hearty mind.

Philippians 3:15-21

15All of us, then, who are mature should take such a view of things. And if on some point you think differently, that too God will make clear to you. 16Only let us live up to what we have already attained.

17Join together in following my example, brothers and sisters, and just as you have us as a model, keep your eyes on those who live as we do. 18For, as I have often told you before and now tell you again even with tears, many live as enemies of the cross of Christ. 19Their destiny is destruction, their god is their stomach, and their glory is in their shame. Their mind is set on earthly things. 20But our citizenship is in heaven. And we eagerly await a Savior from there, the Lord Jesus Christ, 21who, by the power that enables him to bring everything under his control, will transform our lowly bodies so that they will be like his glorious body.

Lesson One: Possessing a hearty mind comes from living with discipline.

In this section Paul continues with the idea of sanctification. He encourages his friends to, "… live up to what we have already attained … (vv15-16). It is not possible for the Christian to lose his salvation; but he can lose rewards along the journey of life (1 Cor. 3:10-15). Paul encourages the Philippians to live disciplined lives, so they do not lose any rewards they have already attained. We, too, must stay focused on the higher goal as we face life and all of its difficulties. God promises to give us everything we need to stay faithful (1 Cor. 10:13).

Lesson Two: Possessing a hearty mind comes from looking to our examples.

Paul stresses the importance of a good example and offers himself as one (v17). He stresses this same point with his friends in Corinth (1 Cor. 11:1). Warren Wiersbe writes, "Of course, Paul is a follower of Christ, so his admonition is not egotistical!"[6] Paul states a simple yet profound truth that permeates his writings: **we need each**

6   Warren Wiersbe. *The Bible Exposition Commentary: New Testament, Vol. II, Ephesians—Revelation*, Colorado Springs, CO: David Cook, 1989: 92.

other! We need to look to those who are strong in the faith. Those who are disciplined in the way of the truth are to be examples for us. The people we choose to associate with matters. Let us find good examples and imitate them. We must also understand: Paul is saying, be a good example. Please remember, just as you look to others, people are looking to you. Do not disappoint those who look to you as an example. Do not let them down. They are counting on you to show them the way. Your life matters in more ways than you can imagine. Live for Jesus, look to those who live for Him, and be someone others can look to as an example for Christ.

Lesson Three: Possessing a hearty mind comes from recognizing those who live contrary to the gospel of Christ and not imitating their selfish ways.

Paul continues with a warning, "For, as I have often told you before and now tell you again even with tears, many live as enemies of the cross of Christ. Their destiny is destruction, their god is their stomach, and their glory is in their shame. Their mind is set on earthly things (vv18-19). Oh friend, please watch out and do not get caught up in the lie pervasive in culture. More will not satisfy you. There is a bumper sticker with the following slogan: "He who dies with the most toys wins." I think it should read: "He who dies with the most toys is dead." We cannot take "things" with us. Do not look for direction from those who live selfishly. Paul writes, "Do not be misled: 'Bad company corrupts good character'" (1 Cor. 15:33). I pass along to you what was once told to me, "Show me your friends and I'll show you your future." If you want a satisfying future look to those who are living for Jesus as an example. Do not chase after things that will one day waste away. Live for Jesus and store up for yourselves treasures in heaven.

Lesson Four: Possessing a hearty mind comes from living with the end in mind.

In the next section of chapter three, Paul encourages his friends to live with the end in mind (vv20-21). He reminds them of their position in Christ. Because they are saved, they are citizens of heaven (v20). This heavenly citizenship guarantees them an eternal reward (v21). We, too, share in this promise. Those of us who are in Christ are just passing through this life. Our home is not here; it is in heaven. This guarantee should consume our thoughts and control our actions. As we cultivate a longing for heaven, we are more likely to consistently live in light of heaven. This is Paul's encouragement: **Live with the end in mind!** Consider the words of James, "You are a mist that appears for a little while and then vanishes" (Js. 4:14b). No matter how long we live on earth, it is a brief moment in light of eternity. We must live with the end in mind. The end as we know it, is the beginning of an eternity in our forever home—heaven. This is why Jesus says, "Do not store up for yourselves treasures on earth, where moths and vermin destroy, and where thieves break in and steal. But store up for yourselves treasures in heaven, where moths and vermin, do not destroy, and where thieves do not break in and steal. For where your treasure is, there your heart will be also" (Mt. 6:19-21). There will be no U-Haul attached to your hearse. Understanding this, how do you develop a healthy and hearty mind?

Response to Chapter Three: (What will you do to develop a hearty mind?)

1. Read Hebrews Chapter 11. What does this chapter teach about looking to the right examples?

_____

_____

_____

_____

_____

_____

_____

_____

_____

_____

_____

_____

_____

_____

_____

_____

_____

_____

_____

_____

_____

_____

Chapter Four

A HOPEFUL MIND

Philippians 4:1-9

1 Therefore, my brothers and sisters, you whom I love and long for, my joy and crown, stand firm in the Lord in this way, dear friends!

2 I plead with Euodia and I plead with Syntyche to be of the same mind in the Lord. 3 Yes, and I ask you, my true companion, help these women since they have contended at my side in the cause of the gospel, along with Clement and the rest of my co-workers, whose names are in the book of life.

4Rejoice in the Lord always. I will say it again: Rejoice! 5Let your gentleness be evident to all. The Lord is near. 6Do not be anxious about anything, but in every situation, by prayer and petition, with thanksgiving, present your requests to God. 7And the peace of God, which transcends all understanding, will guard your hearts and your minds in Christ Jesus.

8Finally, brothers and sisters, whatever is true, whatever is noble, whatever is right, whatever is pure, whatever is lovely, whatever is admirable—if anything is excellent or praiseworthy—think about such things. 9Whatever you have learned or received or heard from me, or seen in me—put it into practice. And the God of peace will be with you.

We are no strangers to worry. Anxiety is a part of our world. This was true in Philippi too (4:6). Perhaps the anxiety in Philippi grows from the discord in the church (4:2). Surely, the opposition Paul and the church face increases the levels of anxiety in the community of faith (1:15-17). Whatever the reasons, Paul's testimony concludes, hope eliminates worry. Hope for those who love Jesus is not dependent on outside circumstances. Hope for the believer is secure. The hope God offers His children is anchored in Christ (Heb. 11:1). This secure hope is what Paul uses to wrap up this joy filled letter. Paul encourages his friends to cultivate a hopeful mind. He urges them to build a mind set on eternal things; one anchored in the hope they have in Christ. This hope is available to us. As we continue in the passage, Paul gives a few important ingredients designed to help build a hopeful mind. The use of these ingredients brings to those who use them a peace that transcends the human mind (vv6-7).

Lesson One: A dynamic prayer life is a key ingredient for building a hopeful mind.

Paul explains, "Do not be anxious about anything, but in every situation, by prayer and petition, with thanksgiving, present your requests to God. And the peace of God, which transcends all understanding, will guard your hearts and your minds in Christ Jesus (vv6-7). Paul teaches his friends the importance of prayer and we must never forget this lesson. Prayer is our weapon against worry. According to *Psychology Today*, most worrying is done after nine o'clock at night. Another survey reveals, more than ninety percent of the things people worry about are not legitimate concerns. In short, many of us worry about things we cannot change, things that are out of our control. In reality, many of us worry for no reason at all. If we are faithful to use the time we normally spend worrying in prayer, we are certain to defeat the enemy and experience the peace of God Paul writes about in this final chapter (vv6-7). Yes, we face a real enemy, the devil; and he is a liar. The Bible teaches our enemy, the devil, is the father of lies (Jn. 8:44). Satan does all he can to keep our minds on things we cannot control. He knows one of the most dangerous things to his plan is a Christian who is faithful in prayer. Oh, brothers, let us be a people who are steadfast in prayer. So, how should we pray? Let me suggest we include four important elements of prayer: Adoration, Confession, Thanksgiving, and Supplication.

Paul encourages his friends to pray away worry. It is the custom of the early church to begin prayer with adoration and confession. Paul teaches his friends, praise and confession are key elements in building a healthy prayer life. The psalmist agrees. He includes exhortations all through the psalms instructing God's children to praise His holy name. Jesus also teaches us to begin our prayer with praise, "Our Father in heaven, hallowed be your name …" (Mt. 6:9). As we seek to pray away worry, let us approach God's mighty throne with adoration. Let us lift Him up with praise. Then we are in a position to confess our sins. Yes, confession is a necessary element in building a healthy prayer life. If we choose to hold onto our sin, David teaches God will not hear our prayers (Ps. 66:18). Confession is not only good for us; it is necessary. We must come clean before God as we pray. And when we freely confess our sins, we can be sure God hears us. We can also be sure, when we confess our sins God forgives us (1 Jn. 1:9). Adoration and Confession are key elements to a healthy prayer life.

Thanksgiving is another important element of prayer (v6). The more time we spend in thanksgiving, the less energy we have to worry. And, remember statistics reveal most of the things we worry about are not legitimate concerns anyway. The devil has a way of getting us to focus on negative things which are not likely to be true. He is a liar. In fact, as earlier mentioned, the devil is not only a liar; he is the father of lies (Jn. 8:44). Do not buy into his lies. Praise God, confess your sins, thank God, and then present your requests to him. Presenting our requests to him is what Paul calls petitions or supplications (v6). This simply means to pray for others and to pray for ourselves, and it should be in this order. We should always pray for others first and then lift up our own concerns. Actually, the more we pray for others the smaller our own concerns grow. Prayer is key in defeating worry. When we pray, we push away worry, and allow the peace of God to fill our minds. A healthy prayer life includes thanksgiving and supplication.

Lesson Two: Thinking on the right things is a key ingredient for building a hopeful mind.

Paul again stresses to his friends the importance of the mind in the Christian life. There will be no *Finding Hope in Hardship* without cultivating a healthy and hopeful mind. The way we think impacts the way we act. Our actions in turn impact the habits we form, and these habits shape our future. If we desire a future filled with joy, we must protect our minds. Consider a sports analogy for a moment. The mind is like the line of scrimmage in a football game. Whichever team controls the line of scrimmage, wins the game. He who controls the mind, wins in life. The mind is the gateway to the heart and whatever makes it into the heart will eventually become our habits. Simply put: (head + heart = habits) is the equation for life. Because the mind is so important, Paul wraps up this section with a list of eight things to think on, *"Finally, brothers and sisters, whatever is true, whatever is noble, whatever is right, whatever is pure, whatever is lovely, whatever is admirable—if anything is excellent or praiseworthy—think about such things* (v8). If we are wise, we will also heed his exhortation.

First, Paul exhorts his friends to think on things which are true. To be true is to be fact. To be true is to be exactly as it appears. It is to be authentic or verifiable. It is to correspond with reality. In biblical context, the final test of truth is God Himself. God is immutable. He does not change. His Word is the written revelation of who He is, and His moral standard of excellence discovered therein is also immutable. God's Word does not change. God is truthful (Titus 1:2) and His Word is true (Jn. 3:33). Therefore, we must think on God's Word. Paul exhorts his friends to meditate on the Scriptures. He writes this to the church in Rome as well (Rom. 12:2). We must meditate on God's Word and allow His truth to shape our minds.

A young boy about five years old wakes up from his nap and begins to climb the bookshelf in the living room. His mom hears a book fall and rushes into the room to find the boy about three shelves high. She notices the bookshelf is about to topple over. Very quickly, she grabs her son and stops the bookshelf from falling. When she asks her son why he was climbing the bookshelf, he points to the big book on top of the shelf. She grabs the big book, dusts it off, and gives it to him. After looking at the book, the boy asks his mother, "What is this book?" The mother replies, "It is the Bible." The boy thinks for a minute and then asks, "What is a Bible?" The mom answers, "It is God's book." The boy thinks again and then replies, "Mom, if it's God's book we should give it back to Him since nobody here uses it." Ouch, that hurts! Unfortunately, this, for many in the American evangelical church today, is a sad reality. Paul's exhortation reminds us this cannot be reality if we are going to build a hopeful mind. We must think on things that are true—God's Word!

The second part of Paul's exhortation is to think on whatever is noble. To be noble is to possess excellent qualities or superior character. In this context, Paul exhorts his friends to think on things of strong reputation. This eliminates many of the conversations taking place in our church hallways. Too often, conversations in our churches revolve around sarcasm, crude humor, the latest movie which is likely filled with ignoble commentary, and issues possessing no eternal value. According to Paul's exhortation, this must change. Our thinking impacts our living and our talking. To the church in Colossae Paul writes, "Let your conversation always be full of grace, seasoned with salt, so that you may know how to answer everyone" (Col. 4:6). We must think on whatever is noble and speak in the same manner.

A new Christian shares how he changed his thought life. He reads different books, listens to different music, watches different programing, and surrounds himself with different people. The fruit of these changes manifests in both his actions and his speech. His conversations are more noble. His speech is "seasoned with salt." As a result, an old friend asks him if he has been "brainwashed." To this my friend replies, "Yes, yes I have been brainwashed!" He goes on to say, his brain needed to be washed because his thinking was not noble, nor were his actions and conversations. Think on things with superior character and excellent qualities.

The third part of Paul's exhortation is to think on whatever is right. To be right in this context is more than just being proper. It is to be in accordance with what is just. To think on whatever is right is to think on the righteousness of God. The righteousness of God is on display in the life of the Lord Jesus Christ. Paul writes, "But now apart from the law the righteousness of God has been made known, to which the Law and the Prophets testify" (Rom. 3:21). Jesus is our example for all things righteous. We are to think on such things and allow these thoughts to influence our behavior and our speech (Heb. 12:1-2).

The fourth part of Paul's exhortation is to think on whatever is pure. To be pure is to be morally pure. Purity is an important part of the Christian life and a theme consistent in Pauline letters. Paul encourages his friends in Corinth to remain pure (2 Cor. 11:2). Paul also challenges young Timothy to keep himself pure (1 Tim. 5:22). To his friends in Ephesus Paul writes, "But among you there must not be even a hint of sexual immorality, or of any kind of impurity, or of greed, because these are improper for God's holy people" (Eph. 5:3). A pure life flows from a pure mind. While most understand, pornography is out of the question; fewer realize the *Bachelor* and many other programs on primetime television should be off limits to the believer. Paul exhorts us to only think on whatever is pure. There is much impurity on "family television" today. Be careful and remember whatever you allow into your mind is likely to come out in your life.

The fifth part of Paul's exhortation is to think on whatever is lovely. The word lovely is not used anywhere else in the New Testament. It means what is attractive or pleasing, not in the sense in which we casually use the term. Paul is not referring to how beautiful a lady looks or how attractive a man may look. Rather, in this context, Paul refers to the antithesis of evil. Literally, Paul is referring to the Lord Jesus and those who reflect Him properly. This is what should entertain our minds. We must think on the Lord Jesus and how He lived His sinless life. The way He loves and the way He lives is lovely, and worthy of imitation. The way He loves and the way He lives should consume our minds and conform our actions.

The sixth part of Paul's exhortation is to think on whatever is admirable. To be admirable is to be of good reputation or to be held in high esteem. In context, Paul is exhorting his friends to think of the good qualities of others. Do not dwell on the negative. See the best in people. This is typical of Paul's view of others. His perspective is shaped by the eternal. He sees people for who they can be with God's help and challenges others to do the same. In first Corinthians chapter thirteen, Paul teaches love is a choice and love chooses to see the best in others. Knowing relationships matter most to God (Mt. 22:36-40) let me encourage you, as you interact with others, to think on what is admirable.

As Paul wraps up this thought, numbers seven and eight on his list are coupled together as if they are a summary of the preceding six things— "if anything is excellent or praiseworthy—think about such things" (4:8). To be excellent is to be of the highest moral character. In context, it means to be like Jesus. Peter agrees, "As obedient children do not conform to the evil desires you had when you lived in ignorance. But just as he who called you is holy, so be holy in all you do; for it is written: 'Be holy, because I am holy'" (1 Peter 14-16). If we are to be excellent, we must put off the old self and put on the new. This will only come from daily walking closely with Jesus.

Praiseworthy, in this context, is anything in which God would approve. Remember, the WWJD (What Would Jesus Do) bracelets? This is a question we can ask to help us think only on whatever is praiseworthy. If Jesus would not do it, then neither should we entertain the thought of doing it. If we ask this simple question before dwelling on and doing things, we would live in a manner that is both excellent and praiseworthy.

Paul exhorts his friends to think on these eight things in order for them to shape their lives. As previously mentioned, thoughts lead to action. Whatever enters your head, will make it into your heart, and these things will then shape your habits. Protect your minds (Rom. 12:2), guard your heart (Pr. 4:23), and let God shape your habits (Ps. 119:11).

Lastly, in this section, Paul writes, "Whatever you have learned or received or heard from me, or seen in me—put it into practice. And the God of peace will be with you" (4:9). Notice, Paul does not ask his friends to do anything he does not already practice himself. Paul understands, the leading cause of atheism are people who profess faith in Christ; but do not possess a growing relationship with Him. This blatant contradiction is something an unbelieving world simply cannot believe. We may be the only picture of Jesus our world ever sees. We need to represent him well. When we do, others benefit, and we experience the abiding presence of the God of peace (4:9).

Philippians 4:10-20

10I rejoiced greatly in the Lord that at last you renewed your concern for me. Indeed, you were concerned, but you had no opportunity to show it. 11I am not saying this because I am in need, for I have learned to be content whatever the circumstances. 12I know what it is to be in need, and I know what it is to have plenty. I have learned the secret of being content in any and every situation, whether well fed or hungry, whether living in plenty or in want. 13I can do all this through him who gives me strength.

14Yet it was good of you to share in my troubles. 15Moreover, as you Philippians know, in the early days of your acquaintance with the gospel, when I set out from Macedonia, not one church shared with me in the matter of giving and receiving, except you only; 16for even when I was in Thessalonica, you sent me aid more than once when I was in need. 17Not that I desire your gifts; what I desire is that more be credited to your account. 18I have received full payment and have more than enough. I am amply supplied, now that I have received from Epaphroditus the gifts you sent. They are a fragrant offering, an acceptable sacrifice, pleasing to God. 19And my God will meet all your needs according to the riches of his glory in Christ Jesus.

20To our God and Father be glory for ever and ever. Amen.

Lesson One: A hopeful mind comes from a place of contentment and is developed over time.

In this section, Paul emphasizes the importance of contentment. He writes to his friends, "… for I have learned to be content whatever the circumstances" (4:11). A keyword in this verse is "learned." Paul makes clear, living in contentment is not automatic for the believer; it is developed over time. He also makes clear; this learning process includes hardship (4:12). Hardship provides the necessary environment for contentment to grow. Paul's life is ladened with difficult times. However, over time he learns to experience contentment in spite of his circumstances. In the oft quoted verse, Paul shares the secret to contentment, "I can do all this through him who gives me strength" (4:13). Jesus is the key to contentment. We will never find what we are looking for in things. True peace, true contentment only comes through the abiding presence of Jesus in our lives.

I vividly remember the first time I experienced this truth firsthand. I had been walking with Jesus for about a year and a half. Bonnie and I were excitedly expecting our first child. We had just opened many gifts from our family for the baby and her nursery. Up to this point in our marriage, we had never really experienced any major challenges. However, on New Year's Eve, Bonnie started having major pains in her stomach. The next day we spent hours at the hospital, and we lost our first baby. The pain was overwhelming at first, and then the joy of the Lord filled my spirit in a way I had never experienced. The peace that transcends our abilities to understand filled my heart, and God gave me the strength to press on in spite of the pain. I do not understand why this happened or why we lost three more babies along our journey, but I do know God is fully in control. I also know God gives peace even in hardship for those who walk closely with Him. Learning to be content is possible for those who rely on the Source— Jesus. Peace is available even in the midst of storms for those anchored in Christ.

Lesson Two: A hopeful mind is possible for those who are generous.

Paul thanks his friends for supporting his ministry from the beginning and continuing to support his efforts while he is imprisoned in Rome. While their past and present support encourage Paul, he is more excited about what their generosity does for them than he is about what their financial support provides for him. Paul knows, it is more blessed to give than to receive (Acts 20:35). He understands, the Philippians will not be poorer for giving to support his ministry. This principle is clear in Scripture and certain to Paul. Paul is also certain the generosity of the Philippians is a sure sign God is at work in their lives. Giving is typically one of the last things believers surrender to God. People will often trust God with their lives; yet hold on to their money. This is not so with the Philippian church. They gave when no other church stepped up to help Paul. Joy fills the heart of the apostle because he knows God is at work in the Philippian church, and he is sure they will be rewarded for their benevolence (Phil. 4:14-18).

Lesson Three: Giving to the work of the gospel results in a promise.

Paul declares a promise to his friends about their needs because of their faithfulness in giving. He writes, "And my God will meet all your needs according to the riches of his glory in Christ Jesus" (4:19). Paul is clear, you cannot out give God. God will meet the needs of His people when they freely give of their resources to support the work of the gospel. Let us be sure we do not confuse needs for "greeds." The promise is to meet the needs of Paul's faithful friends: emotional, spiritual, relational, and financial needs. The promise does not include their greeds: every lust or longing they conjure up. Wishes and wants are not always negative, and they may be received at times, but the promise Paul communicates does not include such things. The promise is clear, when the children of God give obediently in response to the will of God for the work of God to the glory of God their needs will surely be met.

Giving freely and receiving even more may seem like a contradiction for many. However, according to the economy of God, giving does result in receiving. As oxymoronic as this may sound, it is a promise from God's Word. This promise is given "… according to the riches of his glory in Christ Jesus" (4:19). God gives according to His riches, not out of His riches; and His riches are limitless. He lacks nothing in His infinite supply. Consider the following illustration. While walking down the street, you run into a beggar and give him one dollar, yet you have more than fifty thousand in the bank. Your gift to the beggar was out of your supply, rather than according to your supply. The promise of God is according to His riches, not out of His riches. Be encouraged! God's well never runs dry. When you consistently give for the sake of the gospel with a pure heart, you can be sure God will meet all of your needs according to the riches of His glory in Christ Jesus.

Philippians 4:21-23

21Greet all God's people in Christ Jesus. The brothers and sisters who are with me send greetings.

22All God's people here send you greetings, especially those who belong to Caesar's household.

23The grace of the Lord Jesus Christ be with your spirit. Amen.

Lesson One: A hopeful mind understands the value of people.

Paul closes this brief letter with a greeting to "all God's people in Christ Jesus" at Philippi (4:21a). It is clear, Paul values everyone in the church. His love is not simply for the super saints, nor does he withhold his love from those involved in the disputes within the family of faith in Philippi. Paul loves and values all who are "in Christ Jesus." This is an important lesson especially since every church is filled with similar saints. Every church, like the Philippian church, is made of people who think too highly of themselves, people who have the spiritual gift of causing discord, those who are legalistic, others who are more concerned about themselves, and then those who faithfully serve the Lord. Paul expresses his love for all of the Philippians, and we are to follow his example.

Paul continues, "The brothers and sisters with me send greetings" (4:21b). Again, Paul shows the value and love he has for others. Paul acknowledges people matter. Ministry is not a solo journey, and life is not meant to be lived in solitude. We need each other. Solomon agrees, "Two are better than one ..." (Ecc. 4:9). We are better together.

Every saint matters. Paul understands this important truth and lives by the same. He is encouraged by his ministry companions, and he draws strength from their fellowship. This section is not simply a mundane salutation. It is a purpose filled heartfelt closing which places a high value on people and gives a clear picture of Paul's heart. When we love well, *Finding Hope in Hardship* is possible.

Paul's salutation includes, "All God's people here send you greetings, especially those who belong to Caesar's household" (4:22). This final greeting likely includes fellow prisoners, soldiers who are serving as prison guards, household slaves, people of prominence, and family members of the Emperor who heard Paul's testimony of the Lord Jesus Christ. These saints, some newly born, hold a special place in Paul's heart. They also bear testimony of the fruit from the generosity of the Philippians. Again, Paul shows the importance of partnership. Paul clearly expresses, everyone matters.

Lesson Two: A hopeful mind comes from people of grace and lives in a place of grace.

Finally, Paul writes, "The grace of the Lord Jesus Christ be with your spirit. Amen" (4:23). Paul ends the letter the same way he begins the letter with God's grace. He writes, "Grace and peace to you from God our Father and the Lord Jesus Christ" (1:2). Paul writes with joy in the midst of personal challenge. He demonstrates, *Finding Hope in*

Hardship is possible. Even though he cannot know the depth of challenge the Philippians will face as they continue faithfully in the gospel ministry, Paul wishes, in everything and everywhere, his friends will be overwhelmed by the matchless bounty of God's amazing grace which is only found in the Lord Jesus Christ. Paul prays for his friends to walk in grace, to grow in grace, and to extend grace. He hopes for God's grace to fill their hearts and minds, to be in their conversations and relationships, to give them strength for life and ministry, and to carry them through every hardship they will encounter along life's journey.

Lesson Three: A hopeful mind is available to those who believe it is possible.

Paul closes the letter with the word, "Amen" (4:23). The word amen literally means, so be it. Paul expresses a deep conviction that his prayer will be answered. Amen, is a joyful affirmation of Paul's prayer. He is confident the Philippians will indeed experience the grace of God in their coming and their going. Paul firmly believes, *Finding Hope in Hardship* is available to all who walk humbly, give generously, and serve faithfully. May this also be true of you and me, AMEN!

Response to Chapter Four: (What will you do to develop a hopeful mind?)

1. Read Colossians 3:1-17. How is this possible and how does it practically look in life?

   _____

   _____

   _____

   _____

2. Read 1 John 3:16-18; 4:7-21. What do these passages teach about relationships?

   _____

   _____

   _____

   _____

3. Read 1 Corinthians 13:4-8. What do these verses teach about relationships?

   _____

   _____

   _____

   _____

4. Read Ephesians 4:11-12. What do these verses teach about the importance of partnership?

   _____

   _____

   _____

   _____

5. Read Ecclesiastes 4:9-12. What does this passage teach about the importance of relationships?

_____

_____

_____

_____

CONCLUSION

The book of Philippians is an easy read. The average reader can carefully peruse the entire book in less than thirty minutes; yet it is packed with rich precepts and rewarding principles. The life lessons in Philippians are not hidden in deep theological language. These lessons are highly practical and visible to any reader. Time spent reading and studying this joy filled letter is life-changing and necessary for all readers in any generation.

The incarnation and the Deity of Christ are essential doctrines of the Christian faith and the very essence of the book of Philippians. Paul masterfully explains, Jesus is the Christ. He is the Son of God who left heaven and came to earth to live a perfectly obedient life, obedient even to death on a cross. Paul continues, with the glorious resurrection and exultation of Christ. The impact of these preeminent truths is life changing. According to Paul, these truths should change the way we interact with each other and others. These truths should help us live differently especially in difficult times. Jim Talley agrees, "When times seem hopeless and sad, it is good to remember that Jesus went through so much more and carried our burdens so we could find strength and stronger faith in whatever circumstances we find ourselves in."[7] Jesus is the answer to life's questions and the example for life's quest.

Paul demonstrates the importance of prayer throughout the book. This life lesson cannot be overstated. Prayer truly does change things. Prayer does make a difference in our lives and in the lives of those around us. Unfortunately, prayer is often one of the most neglected spiritual disciplines in the church.

Babu and Sally Narendran are medical doctors who run a free medical clinic and an English-speaking school for tribal children in the southern central jungles of India. I visit them regularly. Their testimony is similar to the apostle Paul in the area of prayer. Let me explain: Prayer is a natural part of their everyday life. They pray in the morning, throughout the day, and at night. They pray

---

7   Dr. Jim Talley. "Facebook Post", Dec. 14. Christian Counselor, Oklahoma City, Oklahoma, 2020.

sitting down, kneeling down, walking along the pathway, before seeing patients, while seeing patients, and several other times during their hectic days. Prayer is vital to their lives and to their ministry. They will not let anything keep them from private prayer and prayer time with other believers. Dr. Babu shares of a time they were driving through the forest to a neighboring village. Because of the tough terrain and the potential threat of wild animals, the drive typically takes at least an hour or more. On this day, they ran into a wild elephant. While attempting to escape any danger, Dr. Babu flips his jeep onto its side. Fortunately, the jeep has a top which covers the passengers in both the front and the back of the jeep. While on the jeep's side, Dr. Babu, Dr. Sally, and a few friends start to pray on the side of the road as the elephant draws near. The massive tusks extending from the elephant come within inches of the jeep before the elephant is scared off by another driver. The driver sees the imminent danger, starts blaring his horn, and flashing his lights to scare off the wild animal. Fortunately, the massive elephant runs off into the jungle and everyone escapes without harm. Dr. Babu and the other men flip the jeep upright. They continue their drive to the neighboring village, pray through the night with other believers, and then they return home for a new day of work. Dr. Babu, Dr. Sally, and the other believers value prayer. They also live with a level of joy many others only dream of. Surely, there is a connection. My prayer is for us to be like my friends in India. As the old saying goes, "Let us pray!"

The book of Philippians, albeit a very brief letter, is replete with instructions on the importance of relationships. Paul models and teaches; healthy relationships are significant in *Finding Hope in Hardship* and an important ingredient of the joy-filled life. We really do need each other. The healthier our relationships are the more joy we have in our lives. Jeff Jones agrees, "I'm convinced that our joy quotient is directly related to the quality of our deepest relationships."[8] This is Paul's testimony and should be one of our higher ambitions in life.

The mind matters. Paul places a major emphasis on our perspective. He exercises a positive mind as he writes with such joy while being incarcerated, and he exhorts his readers to think on a list of positive things. This is a theme included in most of Paul's letters. Our thoughts are extremely important; thoughts lead to action! May we be faithful to listen to the apostle and think only on things which are "excellent and praiseworthy."

Service and sacrifice, according to Paul, are hallmark characteristics of a mature Christian and necessary for experiencing joy. Serving others and the sacrificial giving of our time, energy, and resources makes life better for

---

8   Jeff Jones. "LinkedIn Post", December 15, Senior Pastor at Chase Oaks Church, Plano, Texas, 2020.

everyone. When we give, we get what we are truly looking for—joy. Paul teaches, selfishness breeds problems; but selflessness builds people. He encourages his readers to pursue humility and holiness. These attributes strengthen relationships and honor God.

Paul reveals the secret to contentment. There is no ambiguity in his claims. Jesus is the source of true contentment. Things cannot fill the void in the human heart; nor will position or prestige. There is only one thing in which man can find true contentment—a growing relationship with the Lord Jesus Christ. Jesus is the source of contentment. Paul is also clear; Jesus is our source of strength. With His help, we can overcome any and every situation. There is no mountain too high, no river too wide, and no circumstance too dire for those who walk with Jesus daily. With Jesus, we can! It is that simple!

Above all else, in the book of Philippians, Paul teaches the gospel is to be preeminent in the life of the fully devoted follower of Christ. Paul is clear, as recipients of God's grace, we are to be representatives of the same. The apostle calls all of his readers to be ambassadors for the Lord Jesus. Paul does not relegate personal evangelism to the spiritual elite; nor does he delegate it to a few gifted in the area of evangelism. Instead, Paul exhorts all who claim the name of Christ to live life on mission and share the glorious gospel of the Lord Jesus with anyone who will listen. The gospel of Jesus is the only message for the salvation of man. Apart from Christ, man is destined to a real place called Hell. People who die without Christ will spend forever separated from God and His great love. We must share the gospel as often as possible with as many as possible.

ABOUT THE AUTHOR

Shonn is a husband, father and grandfather. He has been happily married to Bonnie since May 22, 1993. They have two daughters. The oldest, Brelin, married Bryce Schubert on December 1, 2018. Bryce and Brelin have a daughter, Indie Eleanor Schubert. Baylee, the youngest daughter, lives at home with her parents. Shonn and the girls serve on staff together at Putnam City Baptist Church in Northwest Oklahoma City. Bryce serves on staff at Crossings Community Church. Bonnie, a retired teacher, faithfully supports Shonn's ministry, mentors their daughters, and helps take care of their granddaughter whenever needed.

Shonn is a life-long student. He has a Bachelor of Arts in Interdisciplinary Studies from the University of South Carolina along with a Master of Arts in Ministry, a Master of Divinity, and a Doctor of Ministry from Luther Rice College and Seminary. Currently, Shonn loves to read and regularly has a book in his hand

Shonn is very active in his community. He volunteers as a Law Enforcement Chaplain for the Oklahoma City Police Department; his love for law enforcement stems from his time in the military. Shonn served in the United States Navy as a Signalman and a Rescue Swimmer.

Shonn is the author of *Go Fish: Reviving Personal Evangelism, The Great Debate: Calvinism or Choice,* and *Maximize Your Leadership*. He is also the co-author of *Hold the Rope: Having a Heart for Jesus.*

Shonn has a big heart for missions. God has allowed him to travel to six of the seven continents, more than 30 countries, and most of the states in the US sharing the gospel of the Lord Jesus, encouraging pastors, and training pastors abroad. He is a mentor to many. More than anything, Shonn loves the Lord with all of his heart and strives to lead others to do the same.

REFERENCES

All Scripture quotations are taken from the New International Version and have been used with permission. The Scripture quotations used can be found on the YouVersion Bible site at https://my.bible.com.

Easley, Jordan, "Facebook Post." Dec. 5. (Pastor First Baptist Church, Cleveland, Tennessee): 2020.

Jones, Jeff, "LinkedIn Post", December 15, (Senior Pastor at Chase Oaks Church, Plano, Texas): 2020.

Menninger, Karl A., "Inspiring Quotes", (https://www.inspiringquotes.us/author/5136-karl-a-menninger).

Spurgeon, Charles Haddon, "Spurgeon at His Best: Over 2200 Striking Quotations from the World's Most Exhaustive and Widely read Sermon Series." (Baker Publishing Group: Ada, Michigan): 1988.

Talley, Jim Dr., "Facebook Post", Dec. 14. (Christian Counselor) Oklahoma City, Oklahoma, 2020.

Tebow, Tebow, "Facebook Post", Dec. 5. (Famous
Football Player and TV personality): 2020.

Tolbert, Malcolm, *Layman's Bible Book Commentary: Philippians,* volume 22, (Broadman Press: Nashville, Tennessee): 1980.

Warren Wiersbe. *The Bible Exposition Commentary: New Testament, Vol. II, Ephesians—Revelation*, (Colorado Springs, CO: David Cook): 1989.

A free ebook edition is available with the purchase of this book.

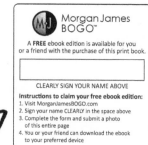
Print & Digital Together Forever.

Snap a photo

Free ebook

Read anywhere

CPSIA information can be obtained
at www.ICGtesting.com
Printed in the USA
JSHW020945280522
26497JS00001B/16

9 781631 956737